THE ROLE OF ISLAM IN THE PUBLIC SQUARE: GUIDANCE OR GOVERNANCE?

The ISIM Papers represent individual lectures delivered at the ISIM. The aim of this series is both to allow the papers, initially presented before limited audiences, to be shared by the entire academic community and to contribute to the further development of the study of Islam in the modern world.

Published by:
International Institute for the Study of Islam in the Modern World (ISIM)

Series Editor:
Dick Douwes

ISIM PAPERS:

1. James Piscatori
   Islam, Islamists, and the Electoral Principle in the Middle East

2. Talal Asad
   Thinking about Secularism and Law in Egypt

3. John Bowen
   Shari'a, State, and Social Norms in France and Indonesia

4. Barbara D. Metcalf
   'Traditionalist' Islamic Activism: Deoband, Tablighis, and Talibs

5. Abdulaziz Sachedina
   The Role of Islam in the Public Square: Guidance or Governance?

FORTHCOMING ISSUE:

6. Lila Abu-Lughod
   Local Contexts of Islamism in Popular Media

THE ROLE OF ISLAM IN THE PUBLIC SQUARE

GUIDANCE OR GOVERNANCE?

Abdulaziz Sachedina
University of Virginia

ISIM PAPER 5

AMSTERDAM UNIVERSITY PRESS
ISIM / LEIDEN

Cover design and lay-out: De Kreeft, Amsterdam

ISBN 90 5356 825 5
ISSN 1568-8313
NUR 717

© Amsterdam University Press, Amsterdam 2006

The Role of Islam in the Public Square: Guidance or Governance?

This ISIM Annual Lecture was delivered on 8 December 2003
at the Academy Building, Leiden University.

In recent decades, especially following the Islamic revolution and the establish-ment of religious authority as the head of government in the modern nation-state of Iran, the public role of religion in general and the role of Islam in par-ticular has been revisited by social scientists. With the American interventions in Afghanistan and Iraq, constitutional debates have as yet to tackle the role of religious convictions and values in the development of democratic institutions to guarantee basic freedoms and rights in those countries. The major stumbling block to democratization appears to be the way the role of religious values is defined in developing an inclusive sense of citizenship without insisting upon doctrinal/theological uniformity. In both of these countries religious leaders have insisted on making the religious law of Islam, the Shari'a, the principal source of defining freedoms and rights in the national constitution. While it is acknowl-edged that in the area of the personal status of a Muslim man and woman, the Shari'a could continue to provide judicial decisions in the area of personal law, there is also a major concern in the way traditional juridical formulations define a woman's social and political rights. More importantly, the religiously pluralis-tic nature of Muslim societies requires taking into consideration not only Sunni-Shi'ite but also interfaith relationships. The need to search for inclusive religious values has assumed a situation of urgency.

The challenge that faces the community today is this: There is a deeply held belief among religiously oriented Muslims that as a comprehensive guide to human life, Islam must not only guide but also govern a modern state with a Muslim majority. Is this conceivable? Are there resources within the classically inherited tradition that can be tapped for the creation of a nation-state that is also a member of the international public order? While the latter question is beyond the scope of the present paper, I want to explore the conceivability of a religious-minded demand in light of the changed circumstances under which modern nation-states conduct their affairs. In order to do that, I will begin my search in the foundational sources of Islamic political discourse in the context in

which this discourse shaped the political underpinnings of the Muslim empire. My reflections on foundational sources like the Qur'an and the Tradition that continue to be held in high esteem by the community will provide me the opportunity to offer my thesis and its ramifications for the democratic governance based on some sort of functional secularity (*sifa madaniyya*). I will return to this secularity later. But let me say this from the outset that I am not imposing this concept on Islamic tradition; rather, separate jurisdictions (*nitaq sulta*), and not the separation of church and state, are acknowledged in the sacred law of Islam, the Shari'a.

Let us examine the interaction between religion and history in Islam. Considering the historical development of Islamic tradition, and contrary to our modern perceptions of the role of religion, one is struck by a religious tradition that has been a source of a public project founded upon the principle of coexistence, recognizing self-governing communities that are free to run their internal affairs under a comprehensive religious and social political system. Of all of the Abrahamic religions based on the biblical ethos of shaping its public culture, Islam has been from its inception the most conscious of its earthly agenda. Islam has been a faith in the realm of the public. The Shari'a regulates religious practice with a view to maintaining the individual's well being through his or her social well being. Hence, its comprehensive system deals with the obligations that humans perform as part of their relationship to the Divine Being and duties they perform as part of their interpersonal responsibility. Public order must be maintained in worship, in the market place, and all other arenas of human interaction. Social transactions based on an ethical standard of conduct in the Shari'a deal with enforcing the law by taking into account only what appears in the public sphere of human interaction. Muslim courts have no jurisdiction over private acts unless infringement of rights occurs and is brought to the attention of the judiciary without prying.[1]

In searching for the guiding principles of a civil society, one must ask whether a faith community can accept the idea that other religious communities have autonomous, self-governing existences. This is the most challenging aspect of one's religious commitment that affects the public order. The essential point to consider is whether religious communities are willing to recognize one another as spiritual equals, each entitled to its own distinctive path of salvation. The reason is that in a democratic pluralistic public order political consensus in the

---

1. Joseph Schacht, *An Introduction to Islamic Law* (Oxford: Clarendon Press, 1964), 189-90 discusses procedure in Muslim courts, observing: "No action is possible without a claimant... This principle is limited by the competence of the kadi to take action in matters of public welfare... It is not compulsory to apply to the kadi... as long as no party applies to the kadi he takes no notice."

public square is dependent upon each group's commitment to inclusive religious convictions.

Here I take religious pluralism to mean the acknowledgement of the intrinsic redemptive value of competing religious traditions. It is expected, however, that beliefs and values essential to one community will contravene those of others; herein lurks the potential for conflict and violence, if religious teachings are not articulated with necessary acumen and practical wisdom in the public square.

The fundamental problem, as reflected in the classical formulation of Muslim political identity, is religious exclusivism founded upon an absolute salvific claim, which runs contrary to the emerging global spirit of democratization through acknowledgment of religious pluralism. At the very core of emerging democratic pluralism is respect for the human rights of the non-Muslims living in Muslim societies. Since the beginning of this century, Muslim religious and social thinkers have wrestled with the issue of Islam's capacity to create a political society that would transcend the traditional boundaries between believers and non-believers and thus allow for the human dignity to emerge as the sole criterion for social and political entitlements under national citizenry.

From its emergence in the seventh century as a tradition in which a prophet is sent as a lawgiver and an organizer of the community to lead it to its ideal existence, Islam has provided its followers with a vision. This vision has something to do with a possibility – a potential – in the public domain of human existence, the possibility of an ideal polity that would shape a Muslim identity for citizens who actively "submit" to the will of God as members of a human community. It is primarily the possibility of appropriating the earth for creating a God-centered multicultural and multiethnic society that animates the Qur'anic vision of interpersonal relations.

It is important to underscore the significance of the Qur'an's universal discourse calling upon humanity to respond to its original nature capable of discerning right from wrong. No human endowed with reason can fail to understand this moral language. More importantly, as a source of unity that transcends religious differences, this language establishes the necessary connection and compatibility between private and particular spiritual, public, and universal moral guidance. Hence, the Qur'an binds all of humanity to its natural predisposition not only to be aware of the meaning of justice but also to will its realization. In this universal idiom, no human being, then, can claim ignorance of the ingrained moral sense of wrong and right; it follows that none can escape divine judgment of a failure to uphold justice on earth.

The Qur'an allows non-believers to be other in the sphere of ethics, where the natural knowledge of good and evil makes injustice in any form inexcusable. No mat-

ter how religions divide people, ethical discourse focuses on human relationships in building an ideal public order. Human relationships at the horizontal level provide us with a framework for defining the religious or cultural other in terms of "we" and "them." Islamic self-identification as a process of self-understanding becomes accessible to the outsider through its conceptual description of the other.

Such a description of the other is situated in the realm of law, the realm of revelation-based religious and moral activity. Islamic law as an expression of the human endeavor to carry out the divine will on earth is actually identical to the belief that faith is an instrument of justice. When law and faith merge in an individual's life, they create a sense of security and integrity about the great responsibility of pursuing justice for its own sake. And when this sense of security and integrity is projected onto the collective life of the community, it conduces to social harmony. Peace, then, is belief translated into action. It is not sufficient merely to believe in justice for peace to come about. Rather, peace is the outcome of justice maintained at each stage of inter-human relations. The separation of law and faith, on the other hand, results in the lack of commitment to justice that leads to chaos, violence, and even war. Hence, the Islamic prescription for avoiding carnage is to respond to God's revelation, which calls for sincere God-human and inter-human relations. In other words, submission to the will of God becomes a kind of conduit for the creation and maintenance of justice and equity on earth. Ultimately, the vision of inter-communal relations in Islam is firmly founded upon the diverse communities' sharing in cross-religious moral concern with egalitarianism, peace, and justice.

But the interaction between this faith and history has not fostered an inter-religious vision of spiritual egalitarianism. In fact, part of the Muslim self-understanding has led to intolerance, even to the exclusion of the other from the divine-human relationship. Such an exclusivist theology can only envision a global human community under Islamic hegemony; Islamic tradition, and so interpreted, becomes an instrument for the furthering of Muslim political and social power over other nations.

However, in a diverse inter-communal society, insistence on agreement on matters of belief as a precondition for social organization is highly problematic. The solution offered by secular liberal theory is that effective governance arises not from shared belief but from a system of government incorporating the principle of religious pluralism. International relations today are conducted without any reference to the substantive beliefs of the member states because religious beliefs are considered "non-public." Whatever their irreconcilable differences in matters of faith, all communities are legally bound to do their part in maintaining peaceful social relations. The resolution of conflicts does not require people to uphold certain religious beliefs; nor does it mean that they do not or cannot share a vision of a future community that is inspired by the belief in transcendence. According to this line of thinking maintained by the political liberalism, judgments based on religious morality are "inaccessible" because "some of the crucial premises that underlie such judgments are not subject of general acceptance or of persuasive demonstration by publicly accessible reasons."[2] As I shall demonstrate in this paper, Abrahamic traditions in general, and Islam in particular, have much to contribute to a discourse about the desirability of including a universal religious argument calling for human cooperation in establishing a just public order.

As a Muslim educated in both the traditional seminary and the modern secular university, I face the unique opportunity and special responsibility of taking up the challenge of a self-critical assessment of current Muslim thought and practice to demonstrate the "accessibility" of religious reasons for developing a necessary "overlapping consensus" in a democratic society for the purposes of just governance.

To begin with, the purpose of revelation is to guide rather than govern humankind. Accordingly, the Qur'anic valuation of human beings is not limited to honoring humankind as the vicegerent of God. It is about believing in the abilities and potential of humankind, the value of time, the authority of the human mind in pursuing the truth, and the future of humankind. The critical evaluation of inequalities between men and women, the degradation of human resources, and the disregard of human experiences provide the Muslim thinker with an opportunity to restate human values in an Islamic context and to restore the balance with other considerations such as national interest, priorities, and traditions.[3]

---

2. Kent Greenawalt, *Religious Convictions and Political Choice* (New York: Oxford University Press, 1988), 68.

3. It is not an easy task for any conscientious Muslim intellectual in the Muslim world or in the West to undertake this critical task without endangering his/her life. The intolerance exhibited by the religious establishment in some Muslim countries and more recently in Muslim communities in Europe and North America, which feels threatened by the rational assessment of religious texts in their historical context in the universities, has forced these scholars to abandon their religious and moral responsibility to their own community. In some cases, these scholars have been forced to go underground and seek asylum in the West. As is well known, both Jewish and Christian academicians have, in the early part of their entry into the academic world, encountered similar reactions from their respective religious authorities and congregations around the world. For Muslims in general, and their communities in the West in particular, the academic study of Islam is a new phenomenon that causes their deep-felt insecurities in faith to react strongly against anything that appears to challenge their long-held belief systems.

By virtue of explicit recognition of a common ground shared between Muslims and the people of the Book, Islam has never harbored a widespread belief that Jews and Christians are to be denied salvation and hence reduced to *persona non grata* status if they do not first convert to Islam.[4] Unlike the early Christians, the early Muslims felt no need to establish their socio-political and religious identity at the expense of another community.[5]

Moreover, Muslims, unlike the Jews, did not regard their own community as uniquely selected to receive divine guidance in a world otherwise bereft of it. Muslims thought of their community as one among many divinely guided communities, all at their beginning equally blessed. Furthermore, as acknowledged in Qur'an 5:48, the Muslims, like various other religious communities, are also an autonomous social organism with their own law for their own members.

CAN RELIGION BECOME A SOURCE OF DEMOCRATIC PLURALISM?

Exclusion of religion as a source of democratic pluralism has been a common tendency in many societies that foster secular values and a clear demarcation between the public and private spheres of human activity. Religion is to be tolerated and even abstractly supported without affording it a clear voice in the public arena because it lacks the ability to communicate with those outside the community.

All world religions, at one time or other, have succumbed to secular pressure and have subordinated their core spiritual-moral message to the political ambitions of their particular communities. Such marriages of convenience between exclusive faith communities and political power has actually led to the disestablishment of the universal ethical and legal foundations of various religious traditions. Abrahamic religions include, among their theological doctrines of divine justice and human moral agency, concepts of individual and collective responsibility to further a divinely ordained ethical public order.

---

4. Karl-Josef Kuschel, *Abraham: Sign of Hope for Jews, Christians and Muslims* (New York: Continuum, 1995), 190.
5. Mark R. Cohen, *Under Crescent and Cross: The Jews in the Middle Ages* (Princeton: Princeton University Press, 1997), 26; Marcel Simon, *Versus Israel: A Study of Relations Between Christians and Jews in the Roman Empire (AD 135–425)* (New York: Oxford University Press, 1986), especially chapter 3.

Thus arises the concentration of comprehensive religious-secular power in the hands of an exclusivist leadership whose views of private morality are divorced from the communalistic vision of society, with the attendant mistreatment of those within and outside the community who reject that community's religious exclusivist claims. Monotheistic communities have from time to time denied their individual members a right to dissent from or reject the communalistic interpretation of their respective traditions because of the fear that such internal dissension (usually labeled apostasy) is potentially fatal to the collective identity of the faith community and its social cohesiveness.

There is a strong desire among the people of various religions to prevent any form of internal dissension. The conflicting and even incommensurable theological positions on freedom of religion in different world communities has led to the oppressive use of force to ensure adherence to a single comprehensive religious doctrine. The ensuing intolerance has manifested itself in intra-faith relationships as well. Whereas Muslims treated other religious communities with relative tolerance, they often treated their own dissenters with extreme cruelty. Thus, for instance, under various powerful Muslim dynasties, the Shi'ite or Sunni minority suffered more oppression than did the Jews and the Christians.[6]

The Iraq-Iran war in the 1980s and the Gulf War in 1990–91 brought home a realization that even secularly based imported ideologies like nationalism and socialism could not advance the cause of pluralistic, tolerant political culture. The imported ideologies, to be sure, were enforced from above without people's rational consent or political participation. Hence, they flagrantly failed to generate the necessary consensus for change in conservative Muslim societies.

---

6. The Shari'a treated the non-Muslim minorities as a special legal category of *ahl al-dhimma*, giving them a status of "protected minorities." And, even when it discriminated against these minorities, their autonomous status as a self-governing community was well-established. On the contrary, there is nothing in the law to guarantee the protection of the life and property of a "dissenter" within the community. A Shi'ite minority was viewed as a "heretical" group by a Sunni majority in power. The situation changed when a Shi'ite dynasty was in power. However, the sheer majority of the Sunni Muslims ruled out the treatment they meted out to the Shi'ite minorities that lived among them. Muslim sources are replete with reports about the execution of the "heretics" (that is, Shi'ite Muslims) who posed a threat to the Sunni governments in power and who openly dissented from the official majority view of Islam. M.G.S. Hodgson, *The Venture of Islam*, 3 vols. (Chicago: University of Chicago Press, 1974) at various points reveals the state policy of the Muslim rule governing its religious minorities. For instance, see: vol. 1:242-51; 305-08; vol. 2:536-39; vol. 3:33-38. The oppressive treatment of Shi'ites continues to this day in a number of Arab and Muslim countries.

The Qur'an does not teach that humanity has fallen through the commission of original sin. But it constantly warns human beings about the egocentric corruption that can weaken the determination to carry out divine purposes for humankind. Human pride can infect and corrupt undertakings in politics, scholarship, everyday conduct, and theology. The last is the most sinful aspect of egocentric corruption because it is done in the name of God.

Besides stressing the "noble nature" (fitra) that promotes human sociability and positive bonds between people because of the common ethical responsibility towards one another, the Qur'an emphasizes the mutual expectations and relations fostered by universal parentage. The Qur'an commands people to honor their parents:

> Thy Lord has decreed that you shall not serve any but Him, and to be good to your parents, whether one or both of them attains old age with thee; say not to them 'Fie' neither chide them, but speak unto them words respectful, and lower to them the wing of humbleness out of mercy and say, 'My Lord, have mercy upon them, as they raised me up when I was little.' (Q. 17:26)

The importance given by the Qur'an to interpersonal relationships evidently points to the institutions and culture that promote the creation of a spiritual-moral community made up of individuals willing and able to take up the challenge of working for the common good. It is for this reason that the moral performance of an individual in society is to be measured not so much by reference to some ingrained "noble nature" as by the religious-moral institutions through which history has shaped the community's ethical aspirations. The doctrine of the "noble nature" (fitra) in the Qur'an is properly anchored in the history of human struggle toward discovering what it is to be properly human.

What of the claim that tolerance leads to a compromise of religious truth? By encouraging tolerance among its members, the community might claim that its transcending quality and its unique relation to truth are sacrificed to pragmatism. Theological differences about any matters in the revelation are difficult, perhaps impossible to resolve. Yet, the spirit of accommodation and tolerance certainly demands that a common ground be sought for implementing the common good in society. Working for the common good without insisting on imposing the beliefs and desires each holds most dear can result in a legitimate public space for diverse human religious experience.

Can this public space be realized without considering ideas about the highest end of human existence on earth? Can they be accomplished through communal cooperation for the collective good or widely different and even irreconcilable individual interests? How can a religious community remain neutral and non-interventionist on ethical issues that from the individual's point of view might run counter to one's sense of the highest end in life?

The secular prescription of Western democracies seems to suggest that religious toleration can be achieved only when the idea of freedom of conscience is institutionalized in the form of a basic individual right to worship freely, to propagate one's religion, to change one's religion, or even to renounce religion altogether. In other words, the principle of toleration is equated with the idea of individual freedom of conscience.[7] Moreover, it restricts the role of conscience to the domain of private faith, which is clearly demarcated from the public realm – hence the separation of church and state. Whereas one has the freedom to choose between competing doctrines and pursue one's belief in private religious institutions, one is linked in common citizenry in public state institutions. This is the secularist foundation of a public order in which, in pursuit of the freedom of conscience, all considerations drawn from a belief in God or other sacred authority in one's private life are excluded from the administration of public life.

Abrahamic traditions are characteristically founded upon the scriptures that locate justice in history through community. This ideal of justice in a divinely ordained community is a natural outcome of the belief in an ethical God who insists on justice and equality in interpersonal relations as part of the believer's spiritual perfection. The indispensable connection between the religious and ethical dimensions of personal life inevitably introduces religious precepts into the public arena. In other words, church and state are closely linked, requiring the involvement of the religious community in taking responsibility for law and order.

FREEDOM OF CONSCIENCE AND RELIGION IN THE QUR'AN

Freedom of conscience and religion has been correctly recognized as the cornerstone of democratic pluralism.[8] Any pluralistic social order requires the active articulation of rational as well as revelational sources of protection for individual autonomy in matters of personal faith within society as part of the divine-human covenant. The question of individual autonomy and human agency might seem

---

7. John Rawls, "The Priority of Right and Ideas of the Good," in *Philosophy and Public Affairs* 17, no. 4: 251-76.
8. Ibid., 260, 265.

peculiar to the modern vision of a public order in which a group of individuals share core ideas, ideals, and values geared towards maintaining a civil society;[9] yet living together in a society requires mutuality not only in matters of commerce and market relations, but it also presupposes a shared foundation of morality and binding sentiments that unite autonomous individuals who are able to negotiate their own spiritual space – and these criteria apply to all societies in all eras.

In general, by virtue of the natural human urge to social interaction, diverse groups fall back on their religious teachings to derive and articulate the rules affecting public life. The recognition and implementation of the religious values of sharing and mutuality creates a civil religion that encourages coexistence with those who, even when they did not share the dominant group's particular vision of salvation, can share in a concern for living in peace with justice. Hence, as I shall contend, the concern for human autonomy, especially freedom of worship (or not to worship), is as fundamental to the Qur'anic vision of human religiosity as it is to that of other civilizations. The Qur'an requires Muslims to sit in dialogue with their own tradition to uncover a just approach to religious diversity and interfaith coexistence. Moreover, a rigorous analysis of the Qur'an will demonstrate that, without recognition of freedom of religion, it is impossible to conceive of religious commitment as a freely negotiated human-divine relationship that fosters individual accountability for one's acceptance or rejection of faith in God, commitment to pursue an ethical life, and willingness to be judged accordingly.

The difference between a moral and religious response to God's guidance is critical here. In relation to the divine purposes for humanity, according to the Qur'an, God provides two forms of guidance: universal moral guidance that touches all humans qua humans, and particular revelatory guidance that is given to a specific faith community. On the basis of universal guidance, it is conceivable to demand uniformity because an objective and universally binding moral standard is assumed to exist that guarantees true human well-being. In enforcing that basic moral standard, resorting to compulsion through legitimate enforcement is justifiable. However, on the basis of particular guidance through scripture, it is crucial to allow human beings to exercise their volition in matters of personal

9. Adam B. Seligman, *The Idea of Civil Society* (New York: Free Press, 1992), chapters 1 and 2 traces the development of the idea in Europe and the United States. The work is not comparative in any sense and therefore does not deal with similar developments in other societies. But, as pointed out in this work, Muslim societies are heir to both biblical and Greek ideas of individual, private, and public realms of human activity. Hence, some of the characteristics that are now identified as being consonant with a civil society have been present in all cultures where people had to learn to live in harmony.

faith because any attempt to enforce religious conviction would lead to its negation. And although the comprehensive nature of scriptural guidance provides a detailed description of ideal human life on earth that is consonant with the historical and cultural considerations of community life in Islam, it removes the God-human relationship from human jurisdiction.[10] So construed, the aspect of revelatory guidance that regulates the God-human relationship is concerned with "reminding" and "warning" people to heed the divine call through "submission" to God's will. As the head of the community, the Prophet could not use his political power to enforce a God-human relationship that is founded upon individual autonomy and human agency. In fact, the Qur'an repeatedly reminds the Prophet that his duty was simply to deliver the message without taking it upon himself to function as God's religious enforcer (Qur'an 17:54; 50:45).

This clarification regarding the two forms of guidance that the Qur'an speaks about provides us with a scriptural basis for freedom of religion. Not only does it maintain the idea of universal and objective moral values that are cognitively accessible to human nature without any distinction between believer and non-believer; it also upholds the notion of a fallible conscience that might fail to respond to God's call. This notion of the possibility of rejecting religious guidance results in the toleration of human autonomy in matters of religious choices.

FREEDOM OF RELIGION IN THE CONTEXT OF ISLAMIC PUBLIC ORDER

But the tension begins as soon as the Qur'an speaks about the just order. There are numerous prescriptive propositions that deal not only with individual reli-

---

10. Michael Walzer, *Thick and Thin: Moral Argument at Home and Abroad* (Notre Dame: University of Notre Dame Press, 1994), pages x-xi uses "thick" to designate the detailed reference to the "particularist stories" across different cultures, which also possess "a thin and universalist morality" that they share with different peoples and cultures. The "thickness" and "thinness" of-the moral tradition of particular peoples and cultures also lead us to recognize the "maximalist" and the "minimalist" meanings, respectively, in that tradition, with a clear understanding that "minimalist meanings are embedded in the maximal morality, expressed in-the same idiom, sharing the same... orientation" (3). I have introduced "universal" and "particular" guidance in the Islamic tradition in a similar conceptual framework, where the-universal provides the minimalist and thin description of the moral principles, whereas the-particular provides the maximalist and thick description of culturally integrated moral language that responds to specific purposes.

gious freedom, but also with the creation of a just social order. I have shown elsewhere how under certain conditions the Qur'an gives the state, as the representative of society, the power to control "discord on earth," a general state of lawlessness created by taking up arms against the established Islamic order.[11] The eradication of corruption on earth, taken in the light of the Qur'anic principle of instituting good and preventing evil, is a basic moral duty to protect the well-being of the community. In Islamic polity, where religion is not divorced from the public agenda, leaving adherents of competing doctrines free to pursue their beliefs engenders an inherent tension between religious communities that has to be resolved through state regulation.

The "millet system" in the Muslim world provided the pre-modern paradigm of a religiously pluralistic society by granting each religious community an official status and a substantial measure of self-government. The system based on the millet, which means a "religiously defined people"[12] was a "group rights model"[13] that was defined in terms of a communitarian identity and hence did not recognize any principle of individual autonomy in matters of religion. And, this communitarian identity was not restricted to identifying non-Muslim "protected minorities" (dhimmis);[14] the millet's self-governing status allowed it to base its sovereignty on the orthodox creed officially instituted by the millet leadership. Under the Ottoman administration, this group status entailed some degree of state control over religious identification, overseen by the administrative officer responsible to the state for the religious community.[15] In addition, the system allowed the enforcement of religious orthodoxy under state patronage, leaving no scope for individual dissent, whether political or religious. Every episode of the individual exercise of freedom of conscience was seen as a deviation from the accepted orthodoxy maintained and enforced by the socio-religious order.

Such an evaluation of the dissent within the Muslim community was also treated with much intolerance that was thoroughly institutionalized in the laws dealing with apostasy and religious rebellion. Juridical studies have shown ample

---

11. Abdulaziz Sachedina, "Justifications for Violence in Islam," in *War and Its Discontents: Pacifism and Quietism in the Abrahamic Traditions*, ed. J. Patout Burns, 122-160 (Washington, DC: Georgetown University Press, 1996).

12. Benjamin Braude, "Foundation Myths of the *Millet* System," in *Christians and Jews in the Ottoman Empire: The Functioning of a Plural Society* (New York: Holes & Meier Publishers, Inc., 1982), 69.

13. Will Kymlicka, "Two Models of Pluralism and Tolerance," in *Toleration: An Elusive Virtue*, ed. David Heyd (Princeton: Princeton University Press, 1996), 82.

14. Braude, "Foundation...," in *Christians and Jews*, 69-72.

15. Ibid.

evidence that Muslim jurists have not engaged in a conceptual investigation of the ethical-legal presuppositions of certain commandments in the Qur'an. In particular, the absence of a thorough analysis of the Qur'anic ethical-legal categories on the one hand, and the ethical-religious on the other, has generated rulings that fail to recognize separate jurisdictions for God-human from human-human relationships. For instance, the Qur'an assigns Muslim public order the obligation of controlling "discord on earth." This phrase is part of a long verse that prescribes the most severe penalties for rebellion:

> The punishment of those who fight against God and His Messenger, and hasten to do corruption, creating discord on earth: they shall be slaughtered, or crucified, or their hands and feet shall alternately be struck off, or they shall be banished from the land. This is degradation for them in this world; and in the world to come awaits them a mighty chastisement, except for those who repent before you lay your hands on them. (Q. 5:33-34)

That the Qur'an presents comprehensive commandments in which moral, religious, and civil are not always easy to distinguish is demonstrated by the equal gravity under civil law accorded to moral and religious transgressions by Muslim jurists.[16] Moreover, Islamic law treats these transgressions as affecting not only humans, but also God. There is a sense in which both humans and God may have claims in the same infringement, even if the event seems to harm only one of them. Although punishment of crimes against religion are beyond human jurisdiction, the juridical body in Islam is empowered to impose sanctions only when it can be demonstrated beyond doubt that the grievous crime included an infringement of a human right (haqq adami, or private claim). The supreme duty of the Muslim ruler is to protect the public interest, a function for which the law afforded him an overriding personal discretion to determine how the purposes of God might best be achieved in the community.

Since criminal law in Islam was a system of private law that fell under the ratifying and enforcement powers of the established political regime, prosecutions for offences like false accusation of unlawful intercourse or theft, crimes that offend against both God's will and just human relations, take place only if initiated by the victim, and the plaintiff must be present both at the trial and execution.[17] In the case of unlawful intercourse, the witness plays a crucial role. There

16. Schacht, *Introduction*, 175-176.
17. Ibid.

must be four witnesses to the actual act of unlawful intercourse. Moreover, at the time of punishment, if the witnesses are not present (and, if the punishment is stoning, if they do not throw the first stones) the punishment is not carried out. If the thief returns the stolen object before an application for prosecution has been made, the prescribed punishment lapses; repentance for highway robbery before arrest causes the punishment to lapse; and if an offence is treated as a misdemeanor (*jinayat*) and the complainant is willing to pardon, blood money may be paid instead or the punishment remitted altogether. In the cases of offenses against religion that are not sanctioned by specific punishments – apostasy, for example (for which there is no defined punishment in the Qur'an) – the effects of repentance are even more far-reaching.

Determining the Role for Islam in Iraq

I do not wish to leave my subject at the level of theory without relating it to the concrete situation dealing with defining the role of Islam in the development of a democratic constitution in Iraq. Off and on there has been a call for integrating the Shari'a in the new constitution in Iraq and Article 2 in the proposed constitution states clearly that Islam will be the "fundamental source of legislation" in a post-Saddam Iraqi state. Religious leaders, mainly Shi'ites, but also some Sunnis, have indicated the Islamic nature of the Iraqi society and the need to make Islamic social and political values part of the overall new political system of Iraq. To assess the seriousness with which this call is made one needs to identify the authority that made the statement. It is not that far-fetched to assert that the religious leadership in Najaf is interested in seeing that the Iraqi constitution reflects the majority view wishing to fulfill the religious dream of situating the Shari'a law at the heart of the political governance.

However, such a call needs to take into consideration fundamental problems that may arise in the Iraqi situation as a modern nation-state. First is the fact of ethnic pluralism that exists in developing a sense of national identity. This also has implications for the development of a democratic constitution in which the notion of citizenship becomes the principle for power distribution. Second is the fact of sectarian plurality that informs religious identities within the broad national culture. This latter identity has gained a heightened sense in the context of enforced Ba'athist secular ideology, over the last three decades. In fact, with favored status of the Sunni community under Saddam, a sectarian identity assumed the source of prime identity in terms of claims and rights that were in many instances denied to the Shi'ites by the Ba'athist government. This entrenched sectarian identity might also become the source of the derailment of any progression towards the democratization of political institutions transcending ethnic and sectarian divide today.

The drafting of the democratic constitution has attempted to address some of the issues that were raised above and which arise out of religious convictions. The question of guaranteeing the rights of non-Muslim minorities has come up quite often in the present deliberations. While it is important to make sure that the new constitution guarantees the fundamental human rights of all citizens, the major issue that needs even more immediate attention is the treatment of women as a "minority." There is a strong possibility that both political as well as religious leaders can disregard Iraqi women's rights. Cultural obstacles are imposed by patriarchal traditionalism that prevails in a religious center like Najaf, whereas discriminatory evaluation of a woman's personal status is enshrined in the inherited juristic law, the Shari'a. Both of these elements can result in the irreparable damage to the status of a woman in the new Iraq, which can deny giving a clear and legitimate voice to women, who constitute over half of the Iraqi population.

Nevertheless, attention must be paid to the cultural sensitivity to anything Islamic in Iraq. Even the atrocious secularism of the Ba'athists could not suffocate this connection of the people with Islamic values. The moderates or reform-minded intellectuals in Iraq, mostly the product of secular education, tend to ignore the popular voices whose loyalty to their religious leaders is unquestioning. The bridge to this connection with the populace today is to provide authentic information on how Islam or Islamic law can or cannot become the source of governance in modern Iraq. Ignoring this important ingredient in building the necessary consensus on how the political system will evolve can actually lead to the rise of militant responses, flared by some of the politically opportunist religious leaders, intent on filling the power vacuum today.

There is little doubt that a fresh understanding of the Shari'a in the public arena should be in place to further its gradual acceptance by the people. Secularism, with its insistence on the separation of "church" and "state" ("seminary" and "state" in Iraqi context), is not responsive to a culture that demands keeping religious values at the core of the emerging national culture. To put it differently, the "disestablishment" of Islam will not work. In fact, not responding to such demands will actually backfire and will be seen as the intentional marginalization of religious institutions and leaders, who are now actively demanding to be heard after a long period of suffocation by the state. At the same time, the main problem that haunts any religious system, including the Shari'a, in a multi-faith situation is its claim to exclusive loyalty. It is worth keeping in mind that, as discussed above, the Shari'a does not advance a concept of egalitarian citizenship – the core of civil rights and responsibilities in a modern nation-state. It simply divides the people into "Muslim members" with full privileges, and "non-Muslim minorities" with a protected status under its divinely ordained system. Furthermore, it ordains laws for both the religious and the socio-political aspects of everyday life. Herein lies the main cause for its incompatibility with the modern democratic system that conceives of its nationals as equal citizens, with equal rights and obligations. More importantly, in the area of gender relationships, the traditional system has instituted inequalities between men and women that could derail the democratic system built on equal rights of all its citizens, regardless of their gender or any other differentiation.

Hence, the Islamic heritage has no paradigm at this time that can offer realistic solutions to the Iraqi situation that are demanded by its ethnically, culturally, and religiously pluralistic population, unless, as demonstrated above, a fresh reading of this heritage is undertaken. Since the majority of the population is Muslim, one can begin to explore the possibilities of retrieving the core values of the Islamic system to offer this fresh Islamic paradigm. This paradigm is actually derived from the religious law of Islam, the Shari'a itself. Let us consider this in the context of Iraq's need for a democratic constitution.

To begin with, we need to search for freedom of religion to enforce an individual's right to adhere to any or none of the confessional communities, without interference from the state. In other words, this is the foundation stone of a democratic Muslim state in which religious freedom to forge one's own spiritual destiny is offered to all citizens without any coercion or discrimination. Is it possible to speak about a human-God relationship in which the state has absolutely no right to intervene or to impose uniformity?

The Shari'a provides the paradigm of a civil religion by separating the jurisdictions (nitaq sulta) in all its laws. I call this a principle of "secularity" (sifa madani-yya). This principle allows religion to manage God's relationship with humanity without interference from any human institutions, including the mosque and the seminary. All those laws that regulate God-human relationships are beyond any adjudication by human courts. There are no penalties for missing the obligations that one performs as part of his/her relationship to God. Only God reserves the right to demand an explanation for such a breach between individual believer and God. This area of the law covers the ibadat – that is, all those actions that are done clearly with the intention of pleasing God.

The second major area of the Shari'a deals with interpersonal social transactions. All laws regulating human relationships are covered under this section.

This area of the law is known as *Mu'amalat* – that is, social transactions that must be conducted between individuals and groups, including the state, in keeping with the demands of justice in all areas of human existence. In this area, human courts have the jurisdiction to enforce its decisions and to demand obedience. More pertinently, it is in this area of the law that reforms affecting social issues have taken place through the reinterpretation of the religious sources. Hence, the theoretical immutability of the sacred law does not get extended to this area.

This separation of jurisdictions is the closest the Shari'a can come to the secularism adopted in Western constitutions. It allows for functional secularity that can generate civic equality and mutual responsibilities at the human-human level of relationship, while maintaining the particularity and independence of the religious tradition from state administration. In other words, the separation of the jurisdictions in Islamic law can respond to the needs of the modern nation-state, where the state must adopt non-interventionist policies in the matter of the religious convictions of its citizens, but guarantee civic equality on the basis of human-human relationships, as required by the Shari'a. More importantly, this aspect of interpersonal relationships could be advanced for the improvement of women's moral and political equality with men, especially when the law concedes that the women have sufficient capacities to enter contracts as equals. In the traditional formulations there is an inconsistency in the law regarding men-women inequalities, which needs to be addressed in terms of the needs of a nation-state committed to democratic values.

Is it reasonable to expect that the fresh adoption of the classical formulations about separate jurisdictions might help carve for Islam an important place in the public arena as the ethical-religious voice of guidance rather than governance? In Iraqi culture it is ultimately the religious authority trusted by the people that can make such a meaning of the Shari'a acceptable. Without the cooperation of religious scholars at this time, it is hard to sell even democracy to the people who are conditioned to the kind of political and religious authoritarianism that prevails in Baghdad and Najaf, respectively. The fear is whether the secular form of authoritarian politics will replace authoritarian religious politics? It is certain that without the cooperation of the moderate religious leadership, Islam in Iraq, especially the version that is heard at the present time, will retain its classical grip of claiming total control over all spheres of human activity to usher in the rule of the uncharted sacred realm. Herein lies the danger to the core democratic values of the civic equality of all citizens in a modern nation-state. The Islamic heritage must guide rather than govern a modern nation-state. Iraq can benefit from its religious heritage provided it treats all of its citizens as "equal in creation." Without this foundation, no political system can claim to be democratic and pluralistic.

CONCLUDING REMARKS

The role of religion in creating the dichotomous relationship between two sens-
es of loyalty – loyalty to one's nation and loyalty to one's religious tradition – is
important in Muslim political culture. The divided loyalty is also a source of two
identities in Muslim consciousness, the identity generated by one's relation to
God, consolidated by one's observance of the sacred law of the Shari'a, and the
identity created by one's experience of living as a member of a corporate body.
The tension arises when the two sources of identities – revelation and reason
– make incompatible and incommensurable demands upon an individual to
hold exclusive and inclusive membership in the community and modern nation-
state, respectively. The solution is provided in the recognition of a principle that
can serve as the foundation for a civil society. This principle can lead the two
identities to converge on a common goal – the overlapping consensus – about
what is the common good in society. Regardless of one's religious affiliation,
the principle, enunciated in one of the administrative documents of classical
Islam, recognizes humans as "equal in creation" and in need of guidance and
not governance from religion to inculcate values that will sustain a meaningful
life. The document was written by the caliph Ali Ibn Abi Talib (d. 660) at the time
when he appointed his governor for Egypt and its provinces. It is important to
bear in mind that Muslim conquerors were in the minority in Egypt. Egypt had
a large Christian population, to whom a proper status had to be granted for
administrative purposes. To reduce the majority to a "non-Muslim" tolerated
people was detrimental to the development of a sense of civic responsibilities
to the conquering Muslim army. In this context, the idea of civic equality was
introduced in the following document written by the caliph himself to underscore the fact that communitarian membership was not incompatible with civic
equality based on human dignity. As long as the role of faith was to instill moral
and spiritual awareness that leads to responsible behavior in society, the governance could be founded upon a more universal principle of recognizing other
humans as one's equal in creation. In other words, the real concern of religion
was to generate respect for all humans as sharing the dignity and honor as God's
creation:

> Infuse your heart with mercy, love, and kindness for your subjects. Be not in face of
> them a voracious animal, counting them as easy prey, for they are of two kinds: *either
> they are your brothers in religion or your equals in creation.* Error catches them unaware,
> deficiencies overcome them, (evil deeds) are committed by them intentionally and by
> mistake. So grant them your pardon and your forgiveness to the same extent that you

hope God will grant you His pardon and forgiveness. For you are above them, and he who appointed you is above you, and God is above him who appointed you. (emphasis added)[18]

The recognition of non-Muslims as "equals in creation" is certainly a status that can be accorded to a citizen regardless of his/her religious affiliation. The role of religion, then, is to foster norms, attitudes, and values that can enhance peaceful relations among different ethnic and religious communities. The norms like "your brothers in religion or your equals in creation" can and should serve as the founding principle of governance through the creation of a civil society.

The question that needs to be addressed is whether a modern society with its pluralistic and diverse citizenry in terms of religious and cultural affiliations can afford to ignore such valuable guidance in matters of its governance of a paradigmatic city of humans "brothers in religion or equals in creation"? The response is very clear in the Qur'an 5:48:

For every one of you [Jews, Christians, Muslims], We have appointed a path and a way. If God had willed He would have made you but one community; but that [He has not done in order that] He may try you in what has come to you. *So compete with one another in good works.* (emphasis added)

It all depends on how the religious communities begin to institutionalize the culture of inclusiveness, realizing that it is truly the divine mystery to allow pluralism in matters of faith and law to exist in human society. What matters ultimately is the common moral responsibility that humans share in order to advance common good.

18. This instruction is part of the famous collection of sermons and letters by Ali b. Abi Talib under the title *Nahj al-balagha*. This translation is rendered by William Chittick in *A Shi'ite Anthology* (London: Muhammadi Trust of Great Britain and Northern Ireland, 1980), 69.

Abdulaziz Sachedina is professor of Religious Studies at the University of Virginia, Charlottesville. Among his publications are the following: *Human Rights and the Conflicts of Culture*, co-authored (University of South-Carolina, 1988); *The Just Ruler in Shi'ite Islam* (Oxford University Press, 1988) and *The Islamic Roots of Democratic Pluralism* (Oxford University Press, 2002).

INTERNATIONAL INSTITUTE
FOR THE STUDY OF ISLAM
IN THE MODERN WORLD (ISIM)

Visiting address:
Rapenburg 59
2311 GJ Leiden
The Netherlands

Postal address:
P.O. Box 11089
2301 EB Leiden
The Netherlands

Telephone:
+31-(0)71-527 79 05

Fax:
+31-(0)71-527 79 06

E-mail:
info@isim.nl

Website:
www.isim.nl